STACK SLASH & SASH
Quilting™

Edited by Carolyn S. Vagts

Annie's

Introduction

Stack, Slash & Sash Quilting is all about creating uniquely beautiful quilts. Create 10 different projects using free-form piecing techniques. Once you've conquered the concept of stacking and slashing blocks, you simply won't be able to stop. The possibilities are endless. Each time you make a quilt using one of these techniques it will be a one-of-a-kind creation.

These amazing quilts are constructed using time saving methods and later trimmed to size. Increasing or decreasing the sizes is easy. Many of the projects could and should be done with existing fabrics. It's a wonderful way to put fabrics to work. The options are limitless. This is a no stress book. You won't have to worry about points and seams aligning. They're not supposed to.

Many use precut fat quarters or strips. So gather up your fabrics, get out your sewing machine and quilting supplies and discover what fun you can have while doing free-form piecing.

Table of Contents

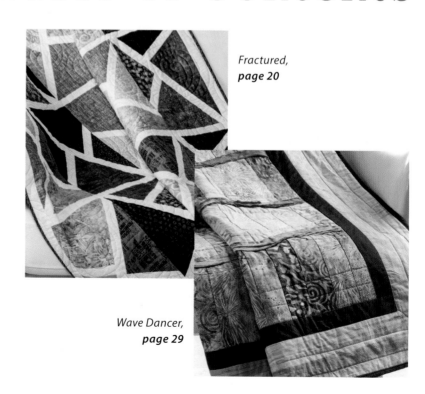

Fractured,
page 20

Wave Dancer,
page 29

Color Me Happy Table Set

Designed & Quilted by Chris Malone

Turn your favorite strips of fabric into gorgeous accents with this unique table set. One table set won't be enough. You'll want to make more.

Specifications
Skill Level: Beginner
Table Runner Size: 50" x 10"
Place Mat Size: 16" x 14"
Napkin Size: 17" x 17"
Napkin Ring Size: 6" x 1½"

Table Runner

Materials
- 20–24 coordinating precut 5" squares
- ⅜ yard coordinating stripe
- ½ yard medium gray solid
- Backing to size
- Batting to size
- Thread
- ½ yard 22"-wide lightweight nonwoven interfacing
- Basic sewing tools and supplies

Project Note
The construction techniques used in this book are meant to produce random results. No two blocks or quilts will look the same, and your results probably will not look like the samples provided.

Finished block and quilt sizes are approximate, and your completed project may not be the same as size listed.

Cutting
From precut 5" squares:
- Cut each square in half to make 40–48 (2½" x 5") A rectangles.

From coordinating stripe:
- Cut 4 (2¼" by fabric width) strips for binding.

From medium gray solid:
- Cut 1 (10½" by fabric width) strip.
  Subcut 4 (8" x 10½") B rectangles.

From interfacing:
- Cut 5 (5" x 11") strips.

Assembly

1. Position one A rectangle right side up on the top edge of an interfacing strip (Figure 1).

Figure 1

2. Layer and pin a second A right side down at an angle on the first A (Figure 2a). Flip second A down to check that it covers the interfacing strip (Figure 2b); rearrange if necessary. Flip piece back up.

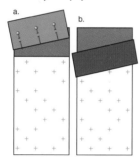

Figure 2

3. Stitch through all layers along second A edge. Trim fabric seam allowance only to ¼" referring to Figure 3. Press second A away from first A.

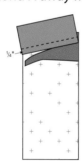

Figure 3

4. Repeat steps adding a third A and reversing the angle (Figure 4).

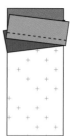

Figure 4

5. Continue in this manner until the interfacing is covered, using approximately eight different A rectangles. Trim the completed pieced A strip to 4½" x 10½" (Figure 5).

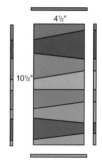

Figure 5

6. Repeat steps 1–5 to make five A strips.

7. Stitch four B rectangles between five A strips into a row referring to the Assembly Diagram; press seams toward B.

8. Sandwich the batting between the pieced top and the prepared backing piece; baste layers together. Quilt as desired.

9. When quilting is complete, remove basting, and trim batting and backing even with raw edges of the pieced top.

10. Prepare binding and stitch to quilt front edges, matching raw edges, mitering corners and overlapping ends. Fold binding to back side and stitch in place to finish.

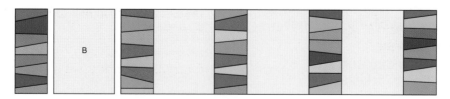

Color Me Happy Table Runner
Assembly Diagram 50" x 10"

Place Mat
(set of two)

Materials

- 12–15 coordinating precut 5" squares
- ⅓ yard coordinating stripe
- 1 yard medium gray solid
- Batting to size
- Thread
- ⅜ yard 22"-wide lightweight nonwoven interfacing
- Basic sewing tools and supplies

Cutting

From precut 5" squares:
- Cut each square in half to make 24–30 (2½" x 5") A rectangles.

From coordinating stripe:
- Cut 3 (2¼" by fabric width) binding strips.

From medium gray solid:
- Cut 1 (14½" by fabric width) strip.
  Subcut 2 (10½" x 14½") B rectangles and
    2 (2½" x 14½") C strips.
- Cut 1 (16" by fabric width) strip.
  Subcut 2 (16" x 18") place mat backings.

From batting:
- Cut 2 (16" x 18") rectangles.

From interfacing:
- Cut 2 (5" x 15") strips.

Assembly

1. Follow Table Runner Assembly steps 1–5 using 5" x 15" interfacing rectangles and approximately 10 A rectangles to make a pieced A strip. Trim strip to 4½" x 14½". Repeat to make a second pieced A strip.

2. Stitch one pieced A strip between B rectangle and C strip to make place mat top referring to Assembly Diagram; press seams away from A. Repeat with remaining A, B and C.

3. For each place mat, sandwich a batting piece between the pieced top and a prepared backing piece; baste layers together. Quilt as desired.

4. When quilting is complete remove basting, and trim batting and backing fabric even with raw edges of the pieced tops.

5. Prepare binding and stitch to quilt front edges, matching raw edges, mitering corners and overlapping ends. Fold binding to back side and stitch in place to finish.

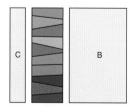

Color Me Happy Place Mat
Assembly Diagram 16" x 14"

Here's a Tip

If you choose to use scraps instead of a purchased collection of precut 5" squares, try to choose prints that have a similar color palette. The actual patterns probably won't be very visible; only the colors need to coordinate.

Napkin & Napkin Ring
(set of two)

Materials
- Remaining A rectangles from table runner and place mats
- ⅝ yard coordinating print
- Batting scraps
- Thread
- Lightweight nonwoven interfacing scraps
- 2 (2⅛"-long) pieces ⅛"-wide elastic
- 2 (¾"-diameter) shank buttons or cover button kits

Cutting

From coordinating print:
- Cut 1 (18" by fabric width) rectangle.
  Subcut 2 (18") napkin squares.
  From remainder of rectangle, cut 2 (2" x 6½") strips for napkin holder backs.

From batting scraps:
- Cut 2 (2" x 6½") strips.

From interfacing scraps:
- Cut 2 (2" x 6½") strips.

Assembly

1. To make napkin ring, follow Table Runner Assembly steps 1–5 using 2" x 6½" interfacing rectangle and 5–7 leftover A rectangles to make a pieced A strip. Trim the edges even with the interfacing. Repeat to make a second pieced A strip.

2. Baste an elastic loop on one end of each pieced A strip (Figure 6).

Figure 6

3. To complete one napkin ring, layer a batting strip, backing, right side up, and a pieced A strip, right side down. Stitch all around, leaving a 2½" opening on one long edge (Figure 7).

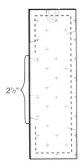

2½"

Figure 7

4. Trim batting close to seam, trim corners and turn right side out. Fold opening seam allowance to inside and slip-stitch closed. Press flat and topstitch ¼" from all edges.

Slipstitch

5. Position and stitch a button to end of napkin holder opposite elastic so the napkin ring ends will meet when button is slipped through elastic loop. *Note: If using cover button kit, follow the manufacturer's directions to cover button with print fabric.*

6. Repeat steps 3–5 to complete second napkin ring.

7. To make one napkin, fold and press ¼" to wrong side of opposite sides of one print 18" square. Fold to wrong side again and press. Edgestitch along first folded edge making a ¼" double-turned hem and referring to Figure 8.

¼" ¼"

Figure 8

8. Repeat step 7 on remaining sides to complete Napkin hem.

9. Repeat steps 7 and 8 to make second Napkin. ■

Color Me Happy Napkin Ring
Placement Diagram 6" x 1½"

Color Me Happy Napkin
Placement Diagram 17" x 17"

"The combination of bright prints with a solid gray reminds me of the weather some days here in the Pacific Northwest—cloudy and dreary until the sun pops through! Colors me happy every time." —Chris Malone

Wonky Flowers

Design by Chris Malone
Quilted by Jean McDaniel

Stitch a colorful flower garden quilt using a fun and easy stacking technique.

Specifications

Skill Level: Confident Beginner
Quilt Size: 65½" x 84½"
Block Size: 8½" x 8½" finished
Number of Blocks: 40

Materials

- 40 (5") precut squares yellow prints
- 8 each (10") precut squares red, blue, pink, aqua, orange and violet tonals and prints
- 2 yards dark green print
- 2 yards light green print
- Backing to size
- Batting to size
- Thread
- 12" square ruler (optional)
- Basic sewing tools and supplies

Here's a Tip

Use leftover 10-inch precut squares for these blocks. Be careful with seam placement and allowances so the pieced blocks can be trimmed to 9" square.

Project Note

The construction techniques used in this book are meant to produce random results. No two blocks or quilts will look the same, and your results probably will not look like the sample provided.

Finished block and quilt sizes are approximate, and your completed project may not be the same as size listed.

Cutting

From light green print:

- Cut 4 (9" by fabric width) strips.
  Subcut 110 (1½" x 9") F sashing strips.
- Cut 8 (2¼" by fabric width) binding strips.

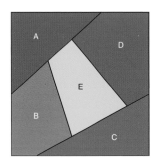

Wonkey Flower
8½" x 8½" Finished Block
Make 40

From dark green print:

- Cut 6 (9" by fabric width) strips.
  Subcut 23 (9") H squares.
- Cut 2 (1½" by fabric width) strips.
  Subcut 48 (1½") G squares.

Assembly

1. Carefully stack four same color family 10" precut squares right side up, matching edges.

Here's a Tip

Cut and assemble one set of four blocks at a time. A stack of four is easy to rotary-cut.

2. Referring to Figure 1a, make two cuts across opposite sides of the stacked squares at different angles. Label pieces A and C and slide away from center shape without disturbing the stacks (Figure 1b).

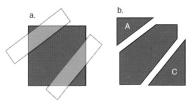

Figure 1

Here's a Tip

It is helpful to use two rulers when making cuts with opposing angles like the A and C cuts in the Wonky Flower blocks. You can move the rulers around until you are happy with the resulting angles and center wedge piece, and then make your cuts.

3. Make cuts at different angles across opposite sides of the center stacked piece to create a wedge shape at the center referring to Figure 2. Label end pieces B and D. Slide A and C back into their original positions.

Figure 2

4. Keeping pieces right side up, remove the top B piece and place it on the bottom of the B stack. Remove the top two C pieces and the top three D pieces and place them on the bottom of the C and D stacks. Lay aside the center wedge pieces for another project. *Note: Rearranging the pieces will create unique blocks with different colored pieces in different places in each block.*

5. To cut the block centers, layer four 5" yellow print squares right sides up. Use a center wedge cut in step 4 as a template and position right side up centered on the yellow print squares and cut four E flower centers (Figure 3).

Figure 3

6. Stitch E between B and D referring to the block diagram; press seams toward B and D.

7. Stitch A and C to the B-D-E unit, keeping A and C corners directly opposite referring to the block diagram; press seams toward A and C.

8. Trim the pieced unit to 9" square to complete a Wonky Flower block.

9. Repeat steps 1–8 with a group of four same color family 10" precut squares and four 5" yellow squares to make a total of 40 Wonky Flower blocks.

10. Arrange and join six H squares, one Wonky Flower block and six F sashing strips to make an X row referring to Figure 4. Repeat to make two X rows. Press seams toward F.

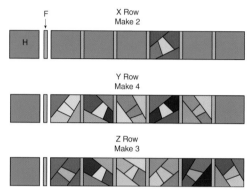

Figure 4

11. Arrange and join two H squares, five Wonky Flower blocks and six F sashing strips to make a Y row, referring again to Figure 4; repeat to make four Y rows.

12. Arrange and join six Wonky Flower blocks, one H square and six F sashing strips to make a Z row, referring again to Figure 4; repeat to make three Z rows. Press seams in rows toward F.

13. Arrange and join seven F strips and six G squares to make a sashing row (Figure 5). Repeat to make 8 sashing rows. Press seams toward F.

Figure 5

14. Arrange block rows and sashing rows referring to the Assembly Diagram for orientation. Press seams in one direction.

13. Sandwich the batting between the pieced top and the prepared backing piece; baste layers together. Quilt as desired.

14. When quilting is complete, remove basting, and trim batting and backing even with raw edges of the pieced top.

15. Prepare binding and stitch to quilt front edges, matching raw edges, mitering corners and overlapping ends. Fold binding to back side and stitch in place to finish. ■

"I love bright colors and anything floral, so when I noticed that the cutting pattern resembled flowers, it was only natural to add a yellow center. The flowers in the border look like they are escaping the flower bed and spreading into the grass!" —Chris Malone

Here's a Tip

You can use a square ruler to square your blocks or position the block on a cutting mat and use a straight ruler in conjunction with the mat grid. Or make a square from template material, center it over the block and trim with a rotary cutter. Just be sure to trim to the indicated size which is ½" larger than the finished block size.

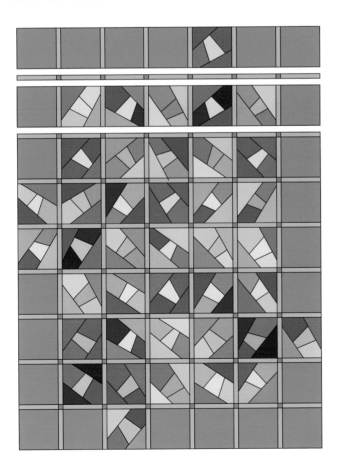

Wonky Flowers
Assembly Diagram 65½" x 84½"

Stack, Slash & Sash Quilting

Pick Up Sticks

Designed & Quilted by Jackie White

Create a progressive image by stacking background blocks by rows and slashing them in different directions. Each row increases by one more slash to create a stunning wall hanging.

Specifications

Skill Level: Intermediate
Quilt Size: 25" x 25"
Block Size: 5½" x 5½" finished
Number of Blocks: 16

Materials

- 7 fat eighths coordinating prints
- ½ yard bold coordinating solid
- 1½ yards white solid or tonal
- Backing to size
- Batting to size
- Thread
- Basic sewing tools and supplies

Project Notes

The construction techniques used in this book are meant to produce random results. No two blocks or quilts will look the same, and your results probably will not look like the sample provided.

Finished block and quilt sizes are approximate, and your completed project may not be the same as size listed.

Here's a Tip

Choose more than six coordinating but different prints for the sticks. Choose a combination of coordinating prints and solids. Or cut 1"-wide strips from scraps at least 10–12" long using a different color family for each block.

Cut extra "stick" strips from fat eighths to provide more choices for combinations of each block.

Use a bold solid for the sashing strips and borders. It will pull together an assortment of prints or scraps.

Cutting

From each fat eighth:
- Cut 8 (1" x 22") B "stick" strips.

From bold coordinating solid:
- Cut 7 (1" by fabric width) C/D/E strips.
    Subcut 12 (1" x 6") C sashing strips.
    Subcut 5 (1" x 24") D sashing and border strips.
    Subcut 2 (1" x 25") E border strips.

From white solid or tonal:
- Cut 3 (7" by fabric width) strips.
    Subcut 16 (7") A squares.
- Cut 3 (2¼" by fabric width) binding strips.

Assembly

1. Stack two A squares right sides up and cut a diagonal slash close to the center of the squares (Figure 1a). Repeat with two more A squares but cut the diagonal slash in the opposite direction (Figure 1b).

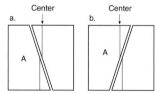

Figure 1

2. Choose one slashed A square. Position and stitch a B strip along the diagonal edge of one section of the A square extending ½" past the A section on each end; press seam toward B (Figure 2).

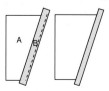

Figure 2

3. Pin-mark the top of the first A section on B as shown in Figure 3.

Figure 3

4. Positioning the top of the diagonal edge of the second A section at the pin on B, match the second A section diagonal and B edges; stitch together (Figure 4). Press seam toward B.

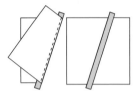

Figure 4

5. Repeat steps 2–4 with remaining slashed A squares, adding a variety of B strips. Trim all pieced A-B units to 6" square to complete four one-"stick" blocks for row 1.

6. Repeat steps 1–4 with four more A squares and a variety of B strips. Do not trim A-B units.

7. Make a second diagonal slash in the opposite direction of the first cut in each A-B unit referring to Figure 5.

Figure 5

8. Insert a B strip between the pieces of the A-B unit lining up the first B strip halves (Figure 6). Press and trim A-B unit to make a 6" square two-"stick" block.

Figure 6

9. Repeat steps 6–8 to make four two-"stick" blocks for row 2.

10. Repeat to make four each three-"stick" blocks for row 3 and four-"stick" blocks for row 4 as shown in Figures 7 and 8.

Figure 7   **Figure 8**

11. Arrange and join the four one-stick blocks with three C strips to make row 1 (Figure 9); press seams toward C. Repeat with remaining blocks and C sashing strips to make the remaining rows referring to the Assembly Diagram.

Figure 9

Here's a Tip

Variety is easy with this design.

• *Switch the background color from white to gray, black or navy.*

• *For a larger quilt, increase the size of the base squares and sashing proportionally.*

• *Larger squares can handle more sticks.*

• *Mix up the blocks instead of ordering them from least sticks to most sticks in rows.*

• *Cut the stick strips in a variety of widths.*

• *Add some fun to the quilt back by using leftover stick strips to piece the quilt back in a similar manner as the front blocks.*

12. Arrange and stitch rows 1–4 together alternately with D sashing strips top to bottom referring to the Assembly Diagram.

13. For borders, stitch a D strip to the top and bottom of the quilt and E strips to opposite sides.

14. Sandwich batting between the pieced top and the prepared backing piece; baste layers together. Quilt as desired.

15. When quilting is complete, remove basting, and trim batting and backing even with raw edges of the pieced top.

16. Prepare binding and stitch to quilt front edges, matching raw edges, mitering corners and overlapping ends. Fold binding to back side and stitch in place to finish. ■

"I was inspired by the clean modern look this quilt gave with hints of color dancing through it. With two boys, my house is never clean, yet in the quilt, the chaos looked fun!" —Jackie White

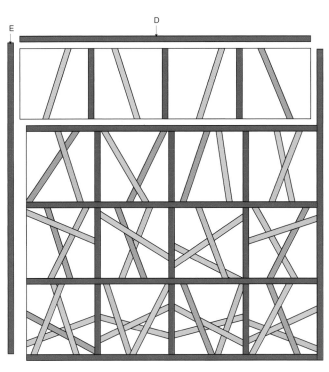

Pick Up Sticks
Assembly Diagram 25" x 25"

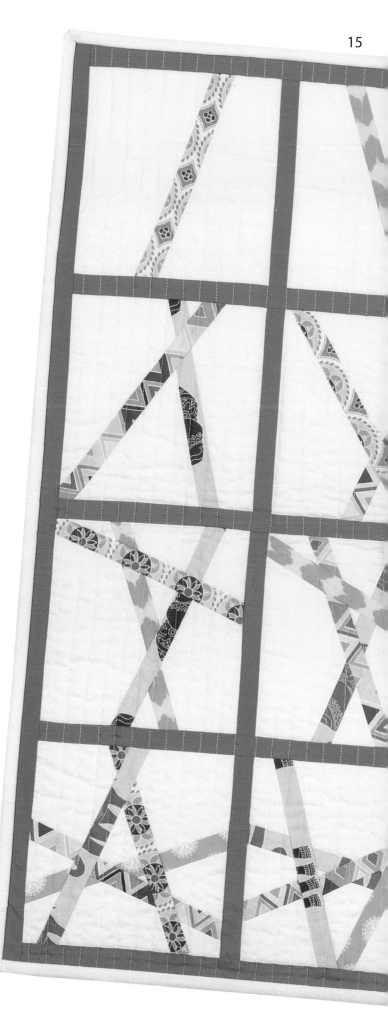

Tidal Waves

Design by Bev Getschel
Quilted by Lynette Gelling

Assorted blue prints cut in gentle curves against a solid background give the illusion of steadily moving waves.

Specifications

Skill Level: Intermediate
Quilt Size: 60" x 85"

Materials

- 6 fat quarters assorted blue and aqua prints
- ⅝ yard coordinating print
- 3⅔ yards white solid
- Backing to size
- Batting to size
- Thread
- 18" x 22" rectangle freezer paper
- Basic sewing tools and supplies

Project Note

The construction techniques used in this book are meant to produce random results. No two blocks or quilts will look the same, and your results probably will not look like the sample provided.

Finished block and quilt sizes are approximate, and your completed project may not be the same as size listed.

Cutting

From coordinating print:

- Cut 8 (2¼" by fabric width) binding strips.

From solid white:

- Cut 2 (60½" by fabric width) lengths.
  Subcut 6 (10½" x 60½") A strips, 2 (5½" x 20½") B strips and 1 (5½" x 10½") C strip.

Assembly

1. With 18" edges at top and bottom, iron fat quarters and stack right sides up. Even up top and bottom edges of fat quarter stack (Figure 1).

Position and iron freezer paper wax side down onto top of stack.

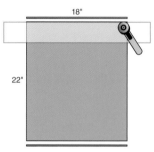

Figure 1

2. Draw gentle curves across the width of the fat quarter stack dividing it into five curved sections (Figure 2). Draw first and last curved lines approximately 4½–5" from the trimmed edges.

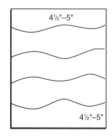

Figure 2

Here's a Tip

Use colored pencils to draw gentle curves on the freezer paper attached to the fat quarters. Remember curves look best if they mirror or echo each other. If you are unhappy with the curves, switch to a different color and redraw. Cut on the colored line you are happy with.

3. Using a new blade in your rotary cutter, cut along the drawn lines and carefully remove freezer paper from top layer of each curved section.

4. To shuffle colors, switch first layer in first section to bottom of layers; switch second layer in second section to bottom. Continue switching layers in this manner for all sections.

5. Choose the top layer piece from each section and arrange on a flat surface with curves matching. Use a removable fabric marker to draw matching marks across the cuts and make ⅛" clips on inside curves referring to Figure 3.

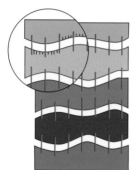

Figure 3

6. Pin and stitch two sections together matching marks (Figure 4). Clip curves again if necessary and press seam flat.

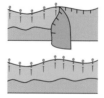

Figure 4

Here's a Tip

Those little marks across the cut edges of the curves are a big deal when sewing the curves together. Even gentle curves can be difficult to match without them.

Generously pin the curves together perpendicular to the seam line matching the marks. Clip the inner curve edges in about ⅛" to provide more give when matching and pinning.

7. Continue to add sections; stitching, clipping and pressing seam flat each time. Assemble six curved rectangles. *Note: The ends of the completed rectangle may be uneven. This will be trimmed later.*

8. Cut three 5½" x 21" D strips from each curve pieced rectangle referring to Figure 5.

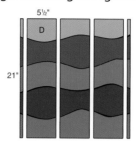

Figure 5

9. Overlap short ends of D strips right sides up. Draw a shallow curve and cut through all layers referring to Figure 6a. Mark and stitch strips together as in steps 5 and 6 (Figure 6b). Press seams open.

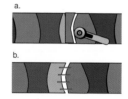

Figure 6

10. Continue to piece D strips together, trimming if necessary, to make two each 5½" x 60½" D1, 5½" x 30½" D2 and 5½" x 10½" D3, and one 5½" x 50½" D4 pieced strips.

11. Stitch D2, B and D3 strips together to make a D-B row referring to Figure 7; press seams open. Repeat to make two rows.

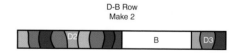

Figure 7

12. Stitch D4 and C together referring to Figure 8 to make one D-C row; press seams open.

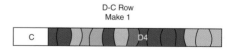

Figure 8

13. Arrange and stitch the A strips and D1, D-B and D-C rows together referring to the Assembly Diagram; press seams open.

14. Sandwich batting between the pieced top and a prepared backing piece; baste layers together. Quilt as desired.

15. When quilting is complete, remove basting and trim batting and backing fabric even with raw edges of the pieced top squaring up quilt if necessary.

Here's a Tip

Quilter Lynette Gelling suggests doubling a border quilting design to fill the white areas with a repeat wave pattern to reflect the designer's theme of this modern quilt.

16. Prepare binding and stitch to quilt front edges, matching raw edges, mitering corners and overlapping ends. Fold binding to back side and stitch in place to finish. ■

Tidal Waves
Assembly Diagram 60" x 85"

"Blue and white are a traditionally fresh and clean combination; in this case they are used in a modern design. The title of this book inspired me. This is a fun technique often used in art quilts." —Bev Getschel

Fractured

Design by Gina Gempesaw
Quilted by Carole Whaling

Stack your rectangles, slash them, add some sashing and repeat. No two quilts will be the same.

Specifications
Skill Level: Confident Beginner
Quilt Size: 49" x 65"
Block Size: 7½" x 14½" finished
Number of Blocks: 24

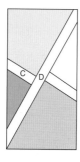

Light Fractured Block
7½" x 14½" Finished
Make 12

Dark Fractured Block
7½" x 14½" Finished
Make 12

Materials
- 12 fat eighths each assorted light to medium gray prints and tonals
- 12 fat eighths each assorted medium to dark gray prints and tonals
- ⅝ yard dark gray print
- 2 yards white tonal
- Backing to size
- Batting to size
- Thread
- Basic sewing tools and supplies

Project Note
The construction techniques used in this book are meant to produce random results. No two blocks or quilts will look the same, and your results probably will not look like the sample provided.

Finished block and quilt sizes are approximate, and your completed project may not be the same as size listed.

Cutting

From light to medium gray prints and tonals:
- Cut 1 (9" x 16") A rectangle from each.

From medium to dark gray prints and tonals:
- Cut 1 (9" x 16") B rectangle from each.

From dark gray print:
- Cut 6 (2¼" by fabric width) binding strips.

From white tonal:
- Cut 2 (6" by fabric width) strips.
  Subcut 48 (1½" x 6") C strips.
- Cut 1 (19" by fabric width) strip.
  Subcut 24 (1½" x 19") D strips.
- Cut 3 (1½" by fabric width) E sashing strips.
- Cut 7 (2½" by fabric width) F/G border strips.

Completing the Blocks
1. With A rectangles right side up, stack four rectangles and cut on the diagonal from top right to bottom left to cut 24 A right triangles (Figure 1).

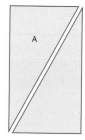

Figure 1

Here's a Tip
When stacking the rectangles, match all outside edges and smooth pieces together. Use a steam iron and press the rectangles together making sure that the stacked pieces do not shift. Keep the stacks together when cutting and arranging the A and B triangles as instructed. Safety pin stacks together or place in separate resealable sandwich bags.

2. Stack four A triangles right side up and cut a random angle from the long angled side to the opposite long edge through all layers referring to Figure 2.

Figure 2

3. Arrange the top section of one A triangle with the bottom section of a different A triangle (Figure 3). Pin triangle sections together. Repeat with all triangles in stack.

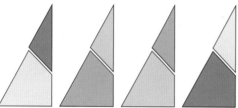

Figure 3

4. Repeat steps 2 and 3 with remaining 20 A triangles.

5. Position and stitch a C strip between a matched pair of A triangle sections, matching the edges of the right angle side and extending C slightly beyond the triangle edges (Figure 4). Repeat to make 24 pieced A-C triangles.

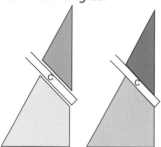

Figure 4

6. Trim the side opposite the right angle even with the bottom triangle section leaving C extended slightly beyond right angle long edge (Figure 5).

Figure 5   Figure 6

7. Position a D strip between two randomly selected A-C triangles and stitch together referring to Figure 6. Repeat with all A-C triangles to complete 12 Light Fractured blocks.

8. Repeat step 1 with B rectangles, cutting on the diagonal from top left to bottom right to cut 24 B triangles referring to Figure 7.

Figure 7

9. Repeat steps 2–7 with B triangles to complete 12 Dark Fractured blocks.

10. Measure all Fractured blocks to determine smallest-size rectangle constructed. Trim all blocks as shown in Figure 8 to the smallest rectangle size. *Note: Drawing shows sample size.*

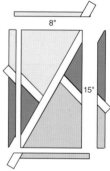

Figure 8

Completing the Quilt

1. Arrange and stitch Light and Dark Fractured blocks alternately in four rows of six blocks each referring to the Assembly Diagram; press.

2. Join the E sashing strips together on short ends. Measure block rows and cut three E sashing strips the same measurement.

3. Stitch E sashing strips between the block rows referring to the Assembly Diagram.

4. Stitch F/G border strips together on short ends with a straight seam. Measure the quilt center referring to Determining Border Lengths on page 31. Cut two each F and G borders the measurements determined.

Here's a Tip

Press seams open throughout this project. Pressing seams open reduces the bulk of the many seams. Also, by pressing the seams open you don't have to worry about the darker fabrics showing through the white sashing strips.

5. Stitch F borders to opposite sides of the quilt and G borders to top and bottom referring again to the Assembly Diagram.

6. Sandwich batting between the pieced top and the prepared backing piece; baste layers together. Quilt as desired.

7. When quilting is complete, remove basting and trim batting and backing even with raw edges of the pieced top squaring up quilt if necessary.

8. Prepare binding and stitch to quilt front edges, matching raw edges, mitering corners and overlapping ends. Fold binding to back side and stitch in place to finish. ∎

"Usually when safety glass breaks, fractures form instead of the glass shattering. The resulting sheet of fractured glass inspired this quilt design." —Gina Gempesaw

Fractured
Assembly Diagram 49" x 65"

Working With Bias Edges

Working with triangles or odd shapes means working with bias edges. While bias edges have a reputation for being difficult to work with, a few tips and a little practice make them more manageable.

The fibers that run either parallel (lengthwise grain) or perpendicular (crosswise grain) to the fabric selvage are straight grain.

Bias is any diagonal line between the lengthwise or crosswise grain (Figure A). At these angles the fabric is less stable and stretches easily. The true bias of a woven fabric is a 45-degree angle between the lengthwise and crosswise grain lines.

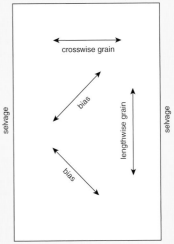

Figure A

A triangle or odd shape will likely have at least one edge that is cut on the bias, so it is even more important to handle the edges with care. You can tell immediately when a bias edge has been mistreated. It will become wavy!

When cutting, keep the fabric flat and move it as little as possible. Even gentle smoothing in place can pull the edges.

Never pull or stretch bias edges when stitching. Slow down and let your sewing machine gently feed the fabric under the needle. It truly doesn't need your help!

Press bias edges with a dry iron. Lift the iron straight up off the fabric, and then move to a new position and lower it straight down. Don't slide the iron over the seam allowances. This can stretch even straight-grain edges.

If you are having trouble with bias edges, you can try starching your fabric before cutting with a laundry starch or, on smaller pieces of fabric, a spray starch. Starching will give the fabric more stability overall.

Creative Curves

Designed & Quilted by Missy Shepler

Try a new technique and turn your experiment into a work of quilted art you can use as a wall hanging. Imagine all the unfinished projects you can revisit and reuse.

Specifications
Skill Level: Confident Beginner
Wall Quilt Size: 18" x 18"
Block Size: 9" x 9" finished
Number of Blocks: 1

Materials
- Medium to large same color family assorted scraps
- ½ yard black solid
- Backing to size
- Batting to size
- Thread
- Basic sewing tools and supplies

Project Note
The construction techniques used in this book are meant to produce random results. No two blocks or quilts will look the same, and your results probably will not look like the sample provided.

Finished block and quilt sizes are approximate, and your completed project may not be the same as size listed.

Cutting
Prewash all fabric before cutting.

From assorted scraps:
- Cut 4 (¾" x 19½") C strips.

From black solid:
- Cut 2 (5" by fabric width) strips.
    Subcut one strip into 2 (5" x 9½") A borders and 1 (5" x 18½") B border.
    From second strip, subcut 1 (5" x 18½") B border. Cut strip remnant in half lengthwise and trim into 2 (2¼" x 23") binding strips.
- Cut 1 (2¼" by fabric width) binding strip.

Completing Center Block
1. Place two fabric scraps right sides up on a rotary-cutting mat, overlapping edges where seam is planned (Figure 1a).

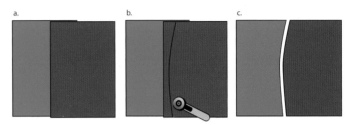

Figure 1

2. Cut a smooth, gentle curve through the overlapped scraps with a small-blade rotary cutter (Figure 1b). Remove the small scraps from the cut area (Figure 1c).

Here's a Tip

Use French curves, which are acrylic shapes used in architectural drafting and dressmaking, as guides to cut smooth curves.

3. Align the cut edges right sides together and stitch using a short stitch length (Figure 2). Clip the seam allowance ¼"–½" apart along the curved edge; press seam allowance to one side.

Figure 2

Here's a Tip

When sewing curved seams, even gentle curves, draw marks across the cut edges of both pieces to use as matching points.

Pin the seam together liberally, matching piece centers, marks and piece ends. Stitch slowly using a short (2mm) stitch length and pivoting as necessary to keep an even seam allowance. Clip the curves as directed.

"I don't like to waste fabric and have a hard time tossing even the smallest scraps. Improv (free-form) piecing allows me to use small scraps and test new designs." —Missy Shepler

Improv Gallery

The center blocks of these small quilts are made by free-form piecing scraps of fabric together. There are no precise measurements, no templates to trace and no patterns to cut. Simply join fabrics to form a 9½" finished block that pleases you. There are no hard and fast rules.

As you might imagine, improvisational or free-form piecing may lead to any number of design ideas and these small scrappy quilts are a great way to test them. Here are a few options for the center block that might inspire your creative side.

Remember! If a piece isn't working, set it aside and start anew. With improv piecing, unfinished items are allowed.

Cut narrow strips from scraps and stitch together lengthwise to create strip sets which can then be cut into sections and re-stitched to make a center block

Cut strips of varying widths, stitch randomly into strip sets, cut sections, flip some sections and re-stitch to make a center block that has the feel of bargello but much less work (Figure A).

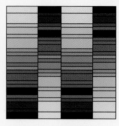
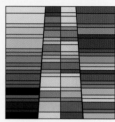

Figure A   **Figure B**

Stitch strip sets and cut into angled sections of different sizes and re-stitch (Figure B).

Stitch curved seams from a single point to make a fan design (Figure C).

Figure C   **Figure D**

Make several small curved-seam units; then, join them to make a larger piece (Figure D).

Insert a narrow section of a solid contrasting fabric between two larger pieced sections (Figure E).

Figure E   **Figure F**

Make perpendicular curved seams for a "wacky patchwork" look (Figure F).

4. Continue adding scraps until the pieced fabric measures approximately 10" square, overlapping previous seams as desired. Square up block to 9½" x 9½" (Figure 3).

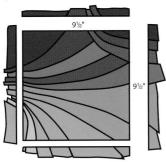

9½"

9½"

Figure 3

Here's a Tip

This technique is easier with larger size scraps. Piece smaller scraps together, pressing seams open, to make larger scraps that can be used as a single unit.

Completing the Quilt

1. Press the C strips in half lengthwise wrong sides together. On right side of center block, align raw edges of a pressed C strip along one side of center block (Figure 4). Baste ⅛" from raw edges to hold. Repeat on all four sides, overlapping C strips at corners.

C

Figure 4

2. Stitch A borders to opposite sides of the center block referring to the Assembly Diagram; press seam allowances toward borders.

3. Stitch B borders to top and bottom of quilt referring to the Assembly Diagram; press seam allowance toward borders.

4. Sandwich batting between the pieced top and the prepared backing piece; baste layers together. Quilt as desired.

5. When quilting is complete, remove basting, and trim batting and backing fabric even with raw edges of the pieced top squaring up quilt if necessary.

6. Make and apply hanger to quilt back as desired, referring to Corner Pocket Hangers.

Corner Pocket Hangers

Small quilts don't need hanging pockets that run across the entire width of the quilt. Make corner hangers by cutting two 6" squares from quilt scraps. Fold diagonally wrong sides together to make two triangles; press.

Align raw edges of triangles with the upper corners of the quilt back before binding but after quilting. Stitch the triangles to the quit corners using a ⅛" seam allowance.

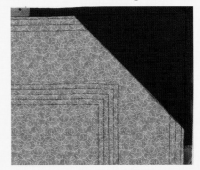

Bind quilt as instructed.

7. Stitch the binding strips together on short ends, inserting 2¼"-wide sections cut from the scraps as desired for an accent.

8. Prepare binding and stitch to quilt front edges, matching raw edges, mitering corners and overlapping ends. Fold binding to back side and stitch in place to finish. ■

B

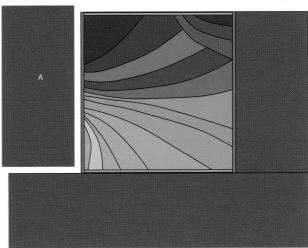

A

Creative Curves
Assembly Diagram 18" x 18"

Wave Dancer

Designed & Quilted by Nancy Vasilchik

Take your strip piecing a step further. Strip piecing, free-form cutting and adding chenille are all that is needed to create this lovely quilt.

Specifications
Skill Level: Confident Beginner
Quilt Size: 48" x 56"

Cutting Bias Strips

Bias strips are cut at a 45-degree angle to the crosswise or lengthwise grain. Strips cut on the bias will have stretch, which makes them perfect for appliqué and other applications where curving the strip is required.

• Cut bias strips from a square that has been cut on the straight grain of the fabric. Handle the edges carefully to avoid distorting the strip edges. Cut strips to total the length needed for your project. An 18" square will yield approximately 144" of 2¼" wide bias strips.

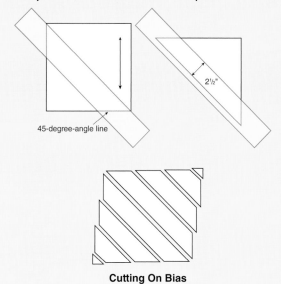

45-degree-angle line

2½"

Cutting On Bias

• Join bias strips with diagonal seams when a continuous strip is needed, like bias binding. Consult your complete guide to quilting for more tips on bias binding.

Materials
• 4 each (2½" by fabric width) precut batik strips from 7 different color groups (28 strips total)
• 6 different batik fat quarters coordinating with precut strips
• ⅞ yard dark solid
• 2 yards coordinating batik
• Backing to size
• Batting to size
• Thread
• Basic sewing tools and supplies

Project Note
The construction techniques used in this book are meant to produce random results. No two blocks or quilts will look the same, and your results probably will not look like the sample provided.

Finished block and quilt sizes are approximate, and your completed project may not be the same as size listed.

Cutting

From batik fat quarters:
• Cut each fat quarter into 2½"-wide bias strips referring to Cutting Bias Strips.
    Keep strips separated in color groups.

From dark solid:
• Cut 5 (2" by fabric width) A/B border strips.
• Cut 6 (2½" by fabric width) binding strips.

From coordinating batik:
• Cut 4 (4½" by fabric length) C/D border strips.

Assembly
1. Select and stitch four precut batik strips together from same color group along length to make a strip set. Repeat to make seven strip sets. Cut each set into five 8½" x 8" units (Figure 1) to total 35 units.

Cut 5
8"

8½"

Figure 1

2. Select and stitch five same color group units together along 8" sides; repeat to make seven long color group sections (Figure 2).

Figure 2

3. Mark a placement line 2" from the top and bottom of each color group section with a fabric marking tool (Figure 3).

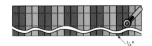

Figure 3

4. Arrange the sections in the order desired top to bottom referring to the Placement Diagram. Cut a free-form wave across the bottom of sections 1–6 between the bottom placement line and the bottom of the section. Keep wave at least ¼" below the placement line and ¼" above bottom edge, referring again to Figure 3.

5. Position top section wave over the straight edge of the second section matching the top section placement line to the second section top edge (Figure 4); pin in place.

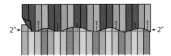

Figure 4

6. Stitch over the raw edge of the wave with a medium-width and -length zigzag stitch through all thicknesses (Figure 5). Trim the underneath section close to the stitching.

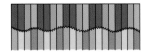

Figure 5

7. Continue to layer and stitch the sections together referring to steps 5 and 6, joining all seven color group sections together to complete the quilt center.

8. Select a color group of bias strips that coordinate with the first wave section. Layer strips together, staggering lengths and overlapping short ends to create a strip set longer than the width of the wave section. Repeat twice to make a stack of at least three overlapped strip sets (Figure 6); baste sets together through the middle lengthwise.

Figure 6

9. Position bias strip stack centered over the wave seam and pin in place referring to Figure 7. Straight-stitch through the middle of bias strips securing them in place and creating a chenille strip that covers the wave seam; remove basting. Repeat over each wave seam.

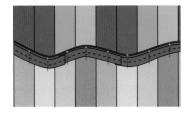

Figure 7

Chenille Strips

To add "froth" to your waves, mimic the fuzzy texture of chenille yarns and fabrics with raw-edged fabric strips sewn over the wave seams.

Because batik fabrics are dense, and the strips are cut on the bias, the fabric strips will fray very little. Regular cotton strips cut on the straight grain will fray more. The less-dense regular cotton should easily follow the gentle curves of the waves and will fray significantly. Choose to use regular cottons for the entire piece or just the chenille strips.

10. Square and trim quilt center if necessary. *Note: Sample was squared to 38" x 45". The dimensions of your quilt will depend on the width of your wave sections which depend on how deep you have cut your waves.*

11. Stitch A/B border strips together on short ends to make one long strip; press seams open. Measure quilt referring to Determining Border Lengths and cut two A side borders. Stitch A borders to quilt center and press seams toward A.

Determining Border Lengths

• To measure for straight borders, lay the pieced quilt top on a flat surface.

• Measure the quilt top through the center from top to bottom and add ½" for seams.

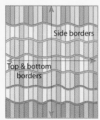

Measuring for Border Lengths

• Measure the quilt top through the center from side to side. Add twice the width of the border plus ½" for seams to this measurement to determine the length to cut the top and bottom borders.

• If making mitered borders, add at least twice the border width to side and top and bottom border lengths and refer to Mitered Borders for construction.

12. Measure and cut top and bottom B borders from remaining A/B strip and stitch to quilt center.

13. Measure quilt again to determine side and top/bottom lengths for C and D borders. Add at least 10" to each length and cut two each C and D borders. Refer to Mitered Corner Borders to apply C and D borders to the quilt.

14. Sandwich the batting between the pieced top and the prepared backing piece; baste layers together. Quilt as desired.

15. When quilting is complete, remove basting and trim batting and backing even with raw edges of the pieced top.

16. Prepare binding and stitch to quilt front edges, matching raw edges, mitering corners and overlapping ends. Fold binding to back side and stitch in place to finish. ■

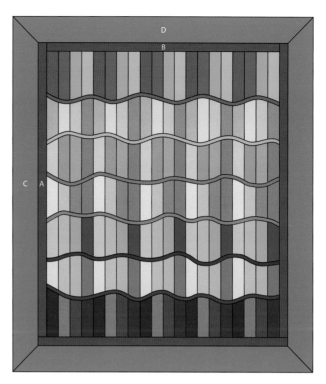

Wave Dancer
Placement Diagram 48" x 56"

Mitered Corner Borders

• Add at least twice the border width to the border lengths measured or instructed to cut.

• Center and sew the side borders to the quilt, beginning and ending stitching ¼" from the quilt corner and backstitching (Figure A). Repeat with the top and bottom borders.

Figure A

• Fold and pin quilt right sides together at a 45-degree angle on one corner (Figure B). Place a straightedge along the fold and lightly mark a line across the border ends.

Figure B

• Stitch along the line, backstitching to secure. Trim seam to ¼" and press open (Figure C).

Figure C

Welcome to My Neighborhood

Design by Jenny Rekeweg
Quilted by Cathie Phillips

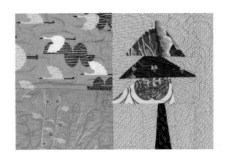

Imagine the young children in your life spending hours playing on this fun floor quilt.

Specifications
Skill Level: Intermediate
Quilt Size: 36" x 36"

Materials
- Assorted large and small scraps prints and solids
- ⅜ yard light brown print
- ⅜ yard medium blue solid
- Backing to size
- Batting to size
- Thread
- Basic sewing tools and supplies

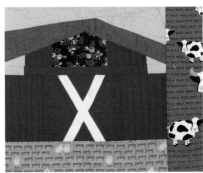

Project Notes
The construction techniques used in this book are meant to produce random results. No two blocks or quilts will look the same, and your results probably will not look like the sample provided. This is especially true of Welcome to My Neighborhood. Customize this quilt to the features of your neighborhood and the background of your family.

Finished block and quilt sizes are approximate, and your completed project may not be the same as size listed. In this quilt, block sizes and number of blocks used are dependent on the theme of each block.

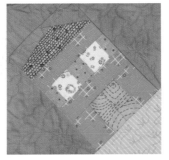
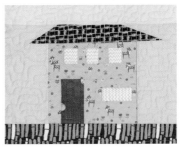

Cutting

From light brown print:
- Cut 4 (2½" by fabric width) strips for road.

From medium blue solid:
- Cut 4 (2¼" by fabric width) binding strips.

Assembly
1. Referring to Jenny's Free-Form Piecing Tips on page 34 and the following block photos, construct blocks as desired.

Jenny's Free-Form Piecing Tips

Here are some tips for creating your own free-pieced quilt with specifics on making Welcome to My Neighborhood from Jenny.

I am a very relaxed quilter who takes "free-piecing" to mean that you make it up as you go! But that doesn't mean I don't rely on some old favorites to get the job done. I use the stack-and-slash method and crazy-quilt techniques to create people, animals, flowers, trees and buildings in my quilts.

For the most part, my ruler is relegated to a straight-edge for my rotary cutter. And I don't rip out seams! I trim and add more or less fabric, sometimes taking a winding path instead of a straight and narrow road to the end.

Planning Your Design

When designing your quilt, decide first what the theme will be and how your quilt will be used. This will guide fabric choices, and quilt and block sizes.

My breakthrough moment with this quilt was deciding on the center block. It grew from there. I had considered a park, a parking lot and a lake. But when I reminded myself to keep it simple, one of my daughter's favorite things was the obvious choice—a rainbow!

After deciding on a finished size, mark that size on your design area in painter's tape. Arrange your completed blocks within this parameter, trimming them to fit or adding other elements to fill the area as you go along.

Welcome to My Neighborhood is approximately 36" square, which is a good size for a child's play mat. It will fit on a bed or on the floor of a small room.

Choosing Fabrics

Begin a free-form project by sorting through your stash—scraps AND yardage.

These projects are a fun way to work through your stash so you can purchase more fabric guilt-free!

Choose some solids to help tone down and tie together what can often be busy blocks.

For Welcome to My Neighborhood, I pulled a number of blue solids for the background. I was pretty sure this would be a busy quilt, so using some solid blues for the sky areas help tone it down and give the eye a place to rest.

Choose other fabrics based on their designs. For example, birds flying, wildflowers or ducks would all evoke certain images that can be worked into blocks.

I even tried to find fabrics for the house rooftops that actually look like shingles and used a fabric that looks like bricks laid out in patterns for the road.

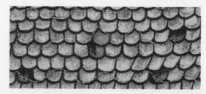

Constructing Blocks

Make each block with an approximate size in mind, so that blocks may have a common measurement but are not exactly the same.

The Welcome to My Neighborhood blocks were started with the idea that they would measure approximately 12½" square, but I really didn't want the quilt to be an even grid. So the branch of road that goes between the trees breaks up the idea of a tic-tac-toe board! The addition of the road also changes square blocks to rectangular.

Planning blocks by sketching your ideas may avert problems during construction but sometimes just going with the flow is great!

I placed the road next to the girl simply because I sewed myself into a pickle and couldn't figure out how to make pickle relish without ripping out a lot of seams! More road strips seemed like a good idea, and I like the happy accident!

1. Divide your blocks into sections that can be easily constructed. Figure 1 illustrates how the Girl block can be divided into four sections: head, arms/hands, skirt and legs/feet. Keep in mind the proportions of each section you are making in relation to the whole design. The legs/feet and skirt take up most of the length of a body so they will be approximately ⅔ of the overall length.

Figure 1

I chose to make the boy and girl larger in scale and out of proportion to the houses because they are just as important of a feature to the quilt.

2. Using two different scrap strips for the leg and foot pieces, stitch the leg to the foot (Figure 2); repeat. Add background scraps between the leg/foot units and on either side to complete the legs/feet section. Trim the top and bottom of the section straight (Figure 3).

Figure 2

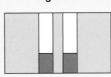

Figure 3

I do not take measurements when I make most of my cuts. I use my rotary blade and mat with a ruler as a straightedge and eyeball the cuts. I keep the widths longer than I expect to need so that positioning the sections together is easier.

3. To make the skirt section, layer a skirt scrap on a background scrap; both scraps should be approximately the width required. Use a ruler and rotary cutter to cut both strips at angles to make the skirt as shown in Figure 4. Remove the cut-away pieces.

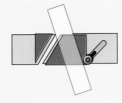

Figure 4

Stacking and slashing works well when constructing elements in blocks that have long, straight edges.

4. Stitch together the skirt and background pieces. Then trim the completed section straight on top and bottom to achieve the desired height (Figure 5).

Figure 5

5. Stitch the skirt section to the legs, positioning as desired (Figure 6).

Figure 6

Since the section widths are not being trimmed, positioning is easy. Slide the sections until you are pleased with how it looks and then stitch. You should have more than enough width.

6. Make the arm width a little narrower than the skirt bottom width. Stitch long hand pieces to both arm ends. Stitch the arms/hands section to the skirt section (Figure 7).

Figure 7

7. To make the head section, begin with a scrap for the face area, stitch and flip hair scraps to the top of the head as shown in Figure 8. As with crazy quilting, trim seam allowances to approximately ¼" wide before adding another scrap.

Figure 8

Some block elements are easier to construct using a crazy-quilt technique rather than stacking and cutting. You can create animals, people, plants and some very odd shapes this way!

8. Stitch and flip background fabric to the head, referring to the red lines in Figure 9, creating the head shape. Make the section at least as wide as the previous sections. Trim the bottom straight and stitch to the arms/hands section to complete the girl unit.

Figure 9

9. Press the girl unit flat and trim all sides straight (Figure 10).

Keep in mind the overall size you would like your blocks to be. Make sure that you trim the block character to a size you can use to create a larger overall block size.

10. Complete the block by adding background to the girl unit and then trim to the block size desired.

Figure 10

Jenny's Free-Form Piecing Tips
Continued

I used the blue as background but added green to the bottom of the block to have sky and grass around the girl. I trimmed the block to fit on point in the quilt corner (Figure 11). This gives the overall circular feel of the quilt design.

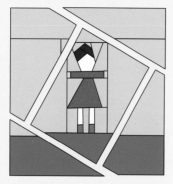

Figure 11

General Tips

Each block will be different, like a jigsaw puzzle, and will need to be adjusted by trimming or adding sashing strips to make each one fit into the quilt parameters. Trimming straight edges for joining blocks is important, but they don't have to be perpendicular unless you want them to be.

Construction should be unregimented, easy and fun! The trees are just wonky Flying Geese units stacked up. The quilt's center rainbow block started in the middle with the pale violet rectangle, and then I simply worked my way around, in sort of an unusual Log Cabin manner. About halfway through, I could tell it was going to be too wide, so I took out some width, but not the height, by using narrower strips on the sides.

Pressing seams open is often the best solution to the number of seam allowances that are made. By pressing seams open, the bulk of the seams is distributed more evenly, which makes quilting easier.

I discussed quilting with my quilter, Cathie Phillips. We decided to add specific elements to the quilting that enhanced the individual blocks. We added butterflies in the sky around the girl, an air balloon behind the boy and panels in the door of one of the houses. This, along with the patterns on the fabrics used, added to the character of each block.

2. Arrange and stitch blocks together in groups with a customized center block, like the rainbow block, at the quilt center referring to the Assembly Diagram. Add 2½" light brown print road strips between the groups to complete the quilt top.

3. Press quilt top on both sides; trim all loose threads. Sandwich batting between the pieced top and a prepared backing piece; baste layers together. Quilt as desired.

4. When quilting is complete, remove basting and trim batting and backing even with raw edges of the pieced top. Square up quilt if necessary.

5. Prepare binding and stitch to quilt front edges, matching raw edges, mitering corners and overlapping ends. Fold binding to back side and stitch in place to finish. ∎

"My own family was the inspiration for this quilt—my son and daughter and all their toys! I can see action figures, cars, trucks and Polly Pocket dolls all at home on this quilt. My husband's family are farmers, so a barn was a necessity!" —Jenny Rekeweg

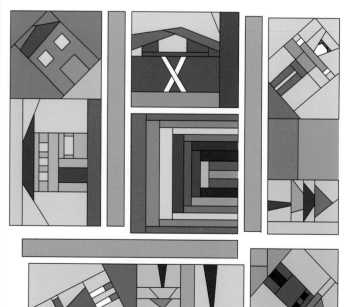

Welcome to My Neighborhood
Assembly Diagram 36" x 36"

Cross My Heart

Design by Jenny Rekeweg
Quilted by Cindi Fletcher of Comforts of Home

Re-create this cross motif over and over with your stash and scraps.
This is the perfect way to turn treasured fabrics into unique quilts.

Specifications

Skill Level: Beginner
Quilt Size: 60" x 77"
Block Size: 9" and 5" finished height by a
   variety of widths
Number of blocks: approximately 80 and 9

Materials

- Assorted scraps for crosses
- For background, choose from same color
  family from either:
     Assorted scraps 6"–10" wide or larger, or
     80–100 (10") precut squares, or
     40–50 fat quarters, or
     6 yards total assorted yardage in ⅜ yard amounts
- Backing to size
- Batting to size
- Thread
- Basic sewing tools and supplies

Project Note

The construction techniques used in this book are meant to produce random results. No two blocks or quilts will look the same, and your results probably will not look like the sample provided.

Finished block and quilt sizes are approximate, and your completed project may not be the same as size listed.

Cutting

From scraps for crosses:
- Cut strips any width and length.

From chosen background fabric (excluding precut 10" squares):
- Cut 10" by fabric width strips and 6" by fabric width strips.
     Subcut strips into a variety of lengths at least 10".

Assembly

1. Refer to Improvisational Crosses on page 40 to make 70–90 Cross My Heart blocks at least 10" high by a variety of widths and 10–12 Cross My Heart blocks at least 6" high by a variety of widths.

Here's a Tip

Adding a row of blocks that finishes 5" high plays nicely into the design. The addition of just one 5" row makes this a nicer length quilt if you are above average in height.

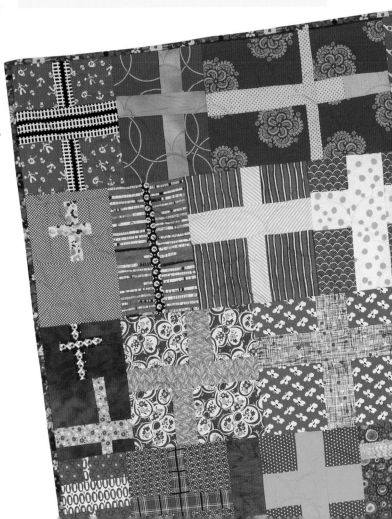

2. Trim top and bottom edges of the larger blocks to make height 9½" (Figure 1a). Trim top and bottom edges of the smaller blocks to make 5½" tall (Figure 1b).

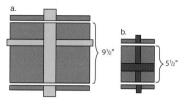

Figure 1

3. Trim opposite sides of all blocks straight. Do not trim to a particular width (Figure 2).

Figure 2

4. Arrange blocks together to make rows approximately the desired quilt width (Figure 3). Arrange eight 9½"-high rows and one 5½"-high row.

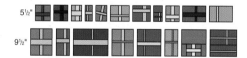

Figure 3

5. If arranged rows are too long, stitch blocks together and then trim the row on one or both ends to the desired width; for example, sample quilt is 60" wide (Figure 4).

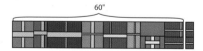

Figure 4

Here's a Tip

Don't make the vertical cross too close to the block edge. The blocks often need to be trimmed at row assembly, and you don't want to worry if a cross shape might be at peril of becoming less like a cross because you needed to trim the background away. Unless, of course, that is what you wanted to do!

6. If arranged rows are too short, add background sashing piece(s) trimmed to 9½" (or 5½" for short row) by width needed between one or more blocks or at the end of the row, referring to Figure 5, to lengthen rows to desired width.

Figure 5

7. Sew rows together in desired order, referring to Assembly Diagram for suggested arrangement.

8. Press quilt top on both sides; trim all loose threads. Square up quilt if needed. Sandwich batting between the pieced top and the prepared backing piece; baste layers together. Quilt as desired.

9. When quilting is complete, remove basting and trim batting and backing even with raw edges of the pieced top.

10. Prepare binding and stitch to quilt front edges, matching raw edges, mitering corners and overlapping ends. Fold binding to back side and stitch in place to finish. ∎

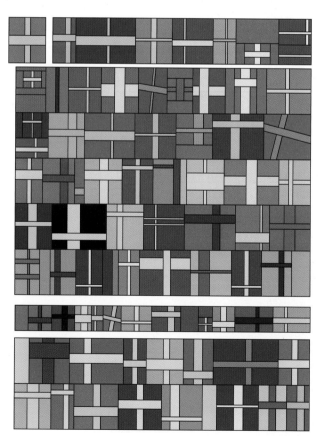

Cross My Heart
Assembly Diagram 60" x 77"

Improvisational Crosses

Putting these blocks together is easy, and they eat up your scraps! Each block is trimmed to the same height but the widths are completely optional before stitching into horizontal rows.

Design Tips

By choosing background fabrics that are in the same color family the scrappy look is less busy. So begin by sorting scraps and stash fabrics by color family and choosing a background color.

Decide on the height of the blocks. All the blocks in a row should be the same height. All rows can be the same height or vary the height of the rows to add another level of interest to the quilt.

Cutting

1. Cut all background fabrics into strips that are slightly larger than the desired height of your blocks by the width of the fabric scrap or yardage.

2. Subcut strips into a variety of widths. It is nice to make a few really wide blocks to make assembly go smoother. It is easier to trim down a very wide block versus adding on to blocks to make rows longer.

3. Choose scraps for the crosses. If not already cut into strips, "free cut" the scraps into strips. That still means cutting with a rotary cutter and ruler to get straight sides for stitching, but it doesn't mean it has to be any specific strip width or length measurement. Variety of both width and length is the key for the cross strips.

Block Construction

1. Begin constructing the blocks with a piece of fabric at least the height of the finished block. Cut it vertically into two pieces as desired (Photo 1).

Photo 1

2. Stitch a cross strip between the two pieces. It is not necessary to match the top edges of fabric pieces. Press seams open (Photo 2).

Photo 2

3. Rotate stitched block 90 degrees and cut vertically for the second cross strip as desired (Photo 3).

Photo 3

4. Stitch the second cross strip together with the block pieces, visually matching the first cross strip pieces. Press seam open (Photo 4).

Photo 4

5. Trim the block to the desired height (Photo 5).

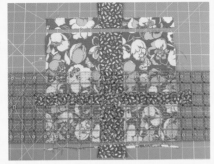

Photo 5

6. Trim the side edges of the block straight for stitching blocks together in horizontal rows (Photo 6).

Photo 6

"As Desired" Block Ideas

The blocks can be as wonky as you desire. Cut the background fabric into uneven pieces or make the vertical cuts at angles (Figure A).

Figure A

Make a smaller block and add background fabric to bring it to the desired size (Figure B).

Figure B   **Figure C**

Stitch two smaller blocks together to make the desired size (Figure C).

Stitch partial crosses or add extra cross strips (Figure D).

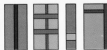

Figure D   **Figure E**

Make a cross float by adding a matching background strip to the block or to the cross strip to extend its length (Figure E).

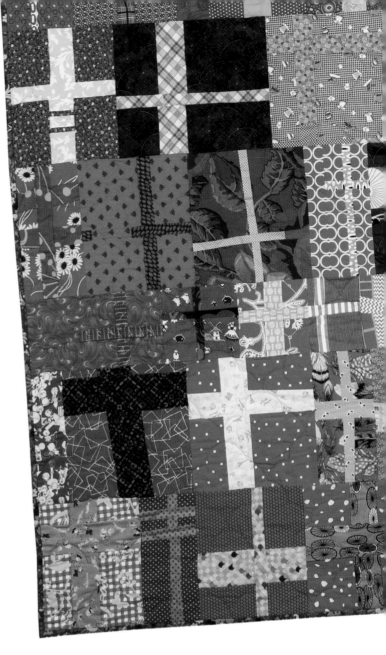

"My favorite free-form or improvisational quilting style is straight edges. No serious thought is required; I just sit down and sew. These blocks are so fun to make; each one is individual and a little masterpiece all on its own. It takes more time than chain-piecing, but it's worth it!" —Jenny Rekeweg

Here's a Tip

This quilt would translate very well into a religious quilt. More traditional-looking crosses would put more emphasis on prayer and hope.

Spooktacular Stacks

Designed & Quilted by CJ Behling

Twelve fat quarters of themed fabrics and a little imagination will give you a spectacular quilt. Anyone would love receiving this beauty.

Specifications
Skill Level: Confident Beginner
Quilt Size: 52" x 66"
Block Size: 14" x 14" finished
Number of Blocks: 12

Materials
- 12 different dark-background Halloween fat quarters
- ⅓ yard lime green print
- 1⅝ yards black with orange dots
- Backing to size
- Batting to size
- Thread
- Glow-in-the-dark thread (optional)
- Basic sewing tools and supplies

Project Note
The construction techniques used in this book are meant to produce random results. No two blocks or quilts will look the same, and your results probably will not look like the samples provided.

Finished block and quilt sizes are approximate, and your completed project may not be the same as size listed.

Cutting

From fat quarters:
- Cut 1 (16½") block base square from each fat quarter referring to Figure 1.

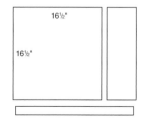

Figure 1

- Cut 4 (1½") C squares from the remainder of one fat quarter.

Spooktacular Block
14" x 14" Finished
Make 12

From lime green print:
- Cut 5 (1½" by fabric width) A/B border strips.

From black with orange dots:
- Cut 6 (4½" by fabric width) D/E border strips.
- Cut 6 (2¼" by fabric width) binding strips.

Completing the Blocks

1. Iron and stack 12 fat quarter squares together matching the raw edges. Write down the fabric order in the stack. ***Note:*** *If you are having trouble cutting 12 layers of fabric at once, cut two 16½" squares of freezer paper and mark the same cutting lines on each. Iron the freezer paper squares to the top of a six layer stack and cut. You will be able to put each section cut together to shuffle a 12 layer stack referring to the chart on page 44.*

2. Referring to Figure 2a, cut diagonally through the fabric stack using your rotary cutter and ruler. Reposition the ruler at another angle and make a second cut. ***Note:*** *Do not move fabrics apart after cutting—gaps in drawing are just for ease of seeing.*

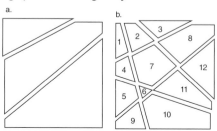

Figure 2

3. Make three more diagonal cuts in the opposite direction as shown in Figure 2b on page 42 to cut the stack into 12 irregular sections. Label the sections, referring to Figure 2b.

4. Shift layers in sections 2–12 from top to bottom of the stack to shuffle the layers. *Note: Refer to Spook Slash & Shuffle below for tips on cutting and shuffling the block base layers to make 12 very different blocks.*

5. Stitch the top layer of sections 1–3 together; press seams toward section 3 to make unit A (Figure 3). Repeat to make a total of 12 units; set aside.

Unit A
Make 12

Figure 3

6. Stitch the top layer of sections 4 and 5 together; press seam toward 5. Stitch sections 6, 7 and 8 together; press seams toward 7. Complete unit B by joining the 4/5 and 6/7/8 sections together referring to Figure 4; press seam toward 4/5. Repeat to make a total of 12 units; set aside.

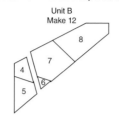

Unit B
Make 12

Unit C
Make 12

Figure 4 **Figure 5**

7. To complete unit C, stitch sections 9–12 together and press seams toward 12 (Figure 5). Repeat to make a total of 12 units.

Spook Slash & Shuffle

These simple tips will help you cut and shuffle your block sections to make blocks that all have one piece of each of the 12 fat quarters and are all very different from each other.

• Iron the block base squares together when stacking. This will help keep the stack from shifting. Stack right side up.

• Be sure you put a new rotary blade in your rotary cutter. You will be cutting through 12 layers when cutting the fat quarter stack.

• If you are having trouble cutting 12 layers of fabric at once, cut two 16½" squares of freezer paper and mark the same cutting lines on each. Iron the freezer paper squares to the top of a six layer stack and cut. You will be able to put each section cut back together to shuffle a 12 layer stack referring to the chart.

• By making five cuts you will cut 12 sections so that each block will contain one section of each fat quarter. Make your cuts on diagonals and at irregular intervals as desired. Draw your cuts on a paper template the size of the block before actually cutting to make sure. If using a character fabric, keep the sections large enough to see the designs you have chosen.

• To shuffle the block sections, label the sections referring to Figure 2b in the Completing the Block instructions; you can mark the numbers on the paper template you made prior to cutting the fabric. Shift the top layer or layers of fabric to the bottom of each section referring to the red numbers in the table below to reorder the fabric layers. By shuffling the fabric layers, each block will contain one section of each of the 12 fat quarters but will be different from every other block.

Section	Shuffle red-number layer(s) to bottom of stack in order shown:
1	Do Not Shuffle
2	2, 3, 4, 5, 6, 7, 8, 9, 10, 11, 12, 1
3	3, 4, 5, 6, 7, 8, 9, 10, 11, 12, 1, 2
4	4, 5, 6, 7, 8, 9, 10, 11, 12, 1, 2, 3
5	5, 6, 7, 8, 9, 10, 11, 12, 1, 2, 3, 4
6	6, 7, 8, 9, 10, 11, 12, 1, 2, 3, 4, 5
7	7, 8, 9, 10, 11, 12, 1, 2, 3, 4, 5, 6
8	8, 9, 10, 11, 12, 1, 2, 3, 4, 5, 6, 7
9	9, 10, 11, 12, 1, 2, 3, 4, 5, 6, 7, 8
10	10, 11, 12, 1, 2, 3, 4, 5, 6, 7, 8, 9
11	11, 12, 1, 2, 3, 4, 5, 6, 7, 8, 9, 10
12	12, 1, 2, 3, 4, 5, 6, 7, 8, 9, 10, 11

• Keep section layers together and chain-piece into block units as instructed. Stitch block units together to complete the blocks.

8. Join the units together as shown in Figure 6 matching seams. Press seams toward unit C or press open to reduce seam allowance bulk. Repeat to make a total of 12 Spooktacular blocks.

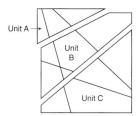

Unit A

Unit B

Unit C

Figure 6

9. Trim and straighten each block to 14½" square as needed.

Completing the Quilt

1. Arrange and join the blocks as desired into four rows of three blocks; press seams in opposite directions between rows.

2. Join rows together, referring to the Assembly Diagram and matching block seams, to complete the quilt center.

3. Join A/B strips together on short ends to make one long strip; press seams to one side. Cut two each 1½" x 56½" A borders and 1½" x 42½" B borders.

4. Stitch C squares to opposite ends of both B border strips.

5. Stitch A to opposite sides of the quilt center referring to the Assembly Diagram; press seams toward A.

6. Stitch B-C borders to the top and bottom of the quilt center referring again to the Assembly Diagram; press seams toward B-C.

7. Stitch D/E border strips together to make one long strip; press seam to one side. Cut two each 4½" x 52½" E borders and 4½" x 58½" D borders.

8. Stitch D to opposite sides of quilt and E borders to top and bottom of quilt ; press seams toward borders.

9. Sandwich the batting between the pieced top and the prepared backing piece; baste layers together. ***Note:*** *You can add a spider to the prepared backing using the Spider appliqué motif included. Refer to the Raw-Edge Fusible Appliqué tips on page 46.*

10. Quilt as desired. ***Note:*** *If you would like to quilt the giant spiderweb and spider, refer to Spooky Quilting.*

Spooky Quilting

To add an even spookier quality to this quilt, quilt it using a giant web and spider design stitched with glow-in-the-dark thread in the top and bobbin. The glow-in-the-dark web absolutely delights little ones (and old ones alike!). Just have fun with this free-form, crazy style and let the web just happen, it will turn out more unique and charming than trying to plan it out.

• Lay the quilt top on a flat surface and mark 6–8 diagonal lines across the quilt for spiderweb spokes referring to Figure A. Then, prepare your quilt sandwich.

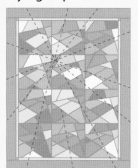

Figure A

• Referring to Figure B, begin by stitching all the web spokes. Then, starting near the intersection of the spokes, stitch curved lines between the spokes in a circular design, stitching 4–6 rounds or until the quilt is covered.

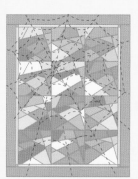

Figure B

• Add a spider to the web where desired. The spider was stitched in the lower right-hand corner of this quilt. Refer to the spider appliqué motif to mark the stitching lines (Figure C).

• If you have added the Spider appliqué to your backing, just stitch around the appliqué pieces using the glow-in-the-dark thread and it will show up on both sides of the quilt.

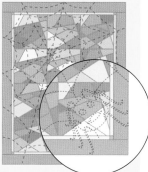

Figure C

• When quilting is complete remove basting and trim batting and backing fabric even with raw edges of the pieced top.

• Prepare binding and stitch to quilt front edges, matching raw edges, mitering corners and overlapping ends. Fold binding to back side and stitch in place to finish.

11. When quilting is complete, remove basting and trim batting and backing even with raw edges of the pieced top.

"I designed this quilt to thrill my son. It definitely worked. If you are really ambitious, you could quilt words or other hidden things in the quilting which, when the lights go out, make for a fun interactive experience with children." —CJ Behling

12. Prepare binding and stitch to quilt front edges, matching raw edges, mitering corners and overlapping ends. Fold binding to back side and stitch in place to finish. ∎

Here's a Tip

Try another version of this quilt using patriotic fabrics. Quilt big bursting fireworks with glow-in-the-dark thread!

Raw-Edge Fusible Appliqué

One of the easiest ways to appliqué is the fusible-web method. Paper-backed fusible web motifs are fused to the wrong side of fabric, cut out and then fused to a foundation fabric and stitched in place by hand or machine. You can use this method for raw- or turned-edge appliqué.

• If the appliqué motif is directional, it should be reversed for raw-edge fusible appliqué. If doing several identical appliqué motifs, trace reversed motif shapes onto template material to make reusable templates.

• Use templates or trace the appliqué motif shapes onto the paper side of paper-backed fusible web. Leave at least ½" between shapes. Cut out shapes leaving a margin around traced lines.

• Follow manufacturer's instructions and fuse shapes to wrong side of fabric as indicated on pattern for color and number to cut.

• Cut out appliqué shapes on traced lines and remove paper backing from fusible web.

• Again following manufacturer's instructions, arrange and fuse pieces on the foundation fabric referring to appliqué motif included in pattern.

• Hand- or machine-stitch around edges. ***Note:*** *Position a light- to medium-weight stabilizer behind the appliqué motif to keep the fabric from puckering during machine stitching. Some stitch possibilities are satin or zigzag, buttonhole, blanket or running stitch.*

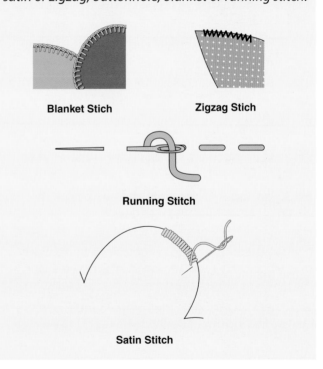

Blanket Stich

Zigzag Stich

Running Stitch

Satin Stitch

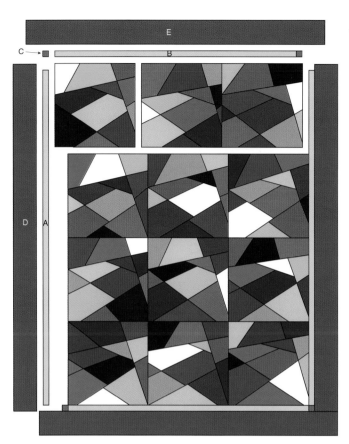

Spooktacular Stacks
Assembly Diagram 52" x 66"

If you add the Spider appliqué to your backing, stitching around the appliqué pieces makes it show up on both sides of the quilt.

Spider appliqué quilt back.

Spooktacular Stacks Back
Placement Diagram 52" x 66"

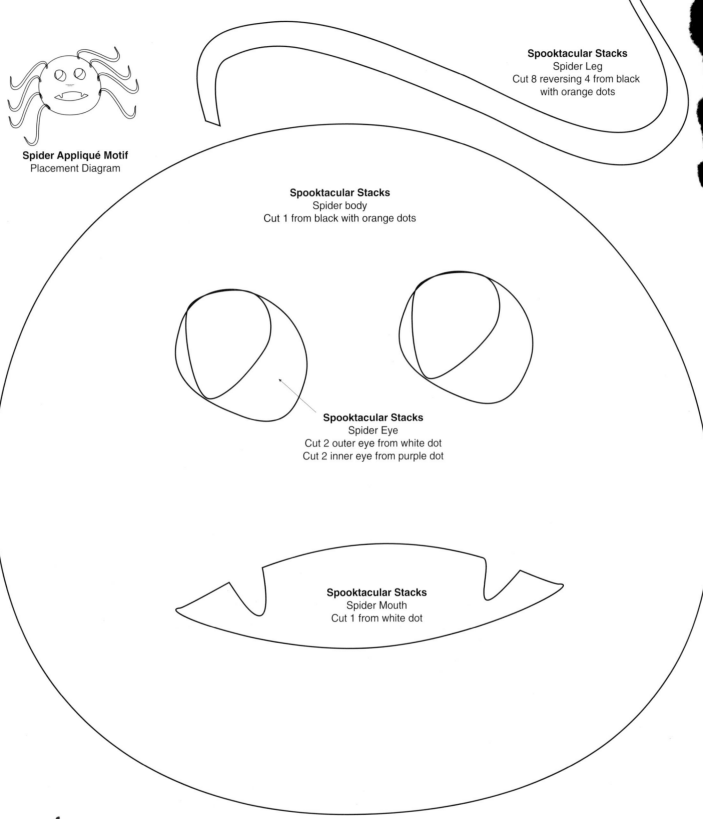

Spider Appliqué Motif
Placement Diagram

Spooktacular Stacks
Spider Leg
Cut 8 reversing 4 from black
with orange dots

Spooktacular Stacks
Spider body
Cut 1 from black with orange dots

Spooktacular Stacks
Spider Eye
Cut 2 outer eye from white dot
Cut 2 inner eye from purple dot

Spooktacular Stacks
Spider Mouth
Cut 1 from white dot

Annie's

ISBN: 978-1-59635-658-0

2 3 4 5 6 7 8 9